Grateful Jake
Resource Guide

by Emily Madill

Grateful Jake Resource Guide © 2012 Emily Madill

ISBN 978-0-9812579-9-0

Library and Archives Canada Cataloguing in Publication

Madill, Emily Elizabeth, 1978-
     Grateful Jake resource guide / Emily Madill.

Accompanies the work: Grateful Jake.
Issued also in electronic format.
ISBN 978-0-9812579-9-0

     1. Gratitude--Study and teaching (Elementary)--Activity programs. I. Title.

BJ1533.G8M33 2012   372.8   C2012-905039-3

Printed in the USA.

Other books by Emily Madill:

***The Captain Joe Collection** ISBN 978-0-9812579-4-5

***Captain Joe to the Rescue** ISBN 978-0-9812579-0-7

***Captain Joe Saves the Day** ISBN 978-0-9812579-1-4

***Captain Joe's Gift** ISBN 978-0-9812579-2-1

***Captain Joe's Choice** ISBN 978-0-9812579-3-8

***Captain Joe Teaching Resources** 978-0-9812579-5-2

TABLE OF CONTENTS

"Gratitude unlocks the fullness of life. It turns what we have into enough, and more. It turns denial into acceptance, chaos to order, confusion to clarity. It can turn a meal into a feast, a house into a home, a stranger into a friend. Gratitude makes sense of our past, brings peace for today, and creates a vision for tomorrow." ~ Melody Beattie

Using the books in the classroom or in a home setting:

I believe introducing children to the concept of gratitude requires more than teaching the appropriate times to say please and thank you. The intention of the Grateful Jake book and the following exercises is to encourage children to begin developing an 'Attitude of Gratitude'. I believe when we view life through the lens of what is working well and take the time to celebrate these things in our lives, we automatically create opportunities to feel confident and motivated. Adopting this kind of valuable outlook can then become an asset and tool children can apply throughout their lives.

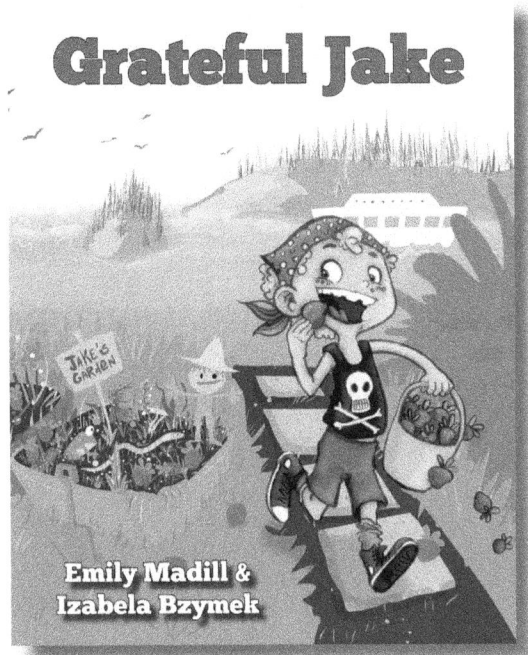

The activities presented in this guide, based on the story Grateful Jake, are intended for a Grade 1 - Grade 3 level of learners, specifically targeting grade 2. If using the activities at home, omit the assessment section. There will be ideas presented for doing each activity at a more individual level in a home setting. The activities could easily be adapted to suit a younger or older learner.

Handouts for the lessons can be found in the Activity Sheets Section. The Activity Sheets Section also contains a Story Sequence handout, Math handout, Word Search, and Spelling Vocabulary List.

There is also a "Comprehension, Word Study and Something to Think About" worksheet in the Activity Sheets section. The Something to Think About question could be used as a journal writing activity. The back of the handout could be used as a space for students to write a longer answer or to illustrate their answer.

Rubrics have been created for some of the lessons as an assessment tool. These Rubrics could be adapted to suit the particular needs of your class. They could also be altered to assess a different learning outcome than the one stated. If using the activities at home, you can omit the assessment section.

Activity #1 - Performing Arts

VISUALIZATION EXERCISE

Lesson Objective/Outcome

To engage learners mentally and prepare them to make pictures in their head (visualize) of things that make them feel happy and they enjoy doing. This activity will help set the foundation for the next activities and help learners start thinking about what they are grateful for in their own lives. .

Preparation and Resources

See Page 48 in Activity Sheets for an easy to read copy of the exercise.

Lesson Idea

<u>HOOK:</u> Read Grateful Jake

IN THE CLASSROOM

Organize students so they are in a safe, comfortable and quiet environment. Have the students close their eyes and lead them through the visualization exercise.

(Note: there is a point form, easy to read and easy to photocopy version of the exercise in the Activity Sheets Section)

FROM HOME

Find a comfortable place, perhaps child's bedroom with their favorite blanket/toy or in a regular gathering place/family room where it is quiet. Ask the child to close their eyes and lead them through the visualization exercise.

Visualization Exercise:

- Close your eyes and imagine you are just waking up in the morning from a long, comfortable sleep. You stretch your arms high above your head as you let out a long yawn.
- Look around your bedroom, what do you see? Do you have some favorite toys or things that are just for you that you keep in your room?
- Keeping your thoughts to yourself for just right now... Pick up one of your favorite toys and bring it with you as you walk to your kitchen where your breakfast is ready, waiting for you to enjoy.
- Keeping your eyes closed for now, think of how happy you feel to see your favorite breakfast. What does your breakfast look like? What does it taste like? Do you eat your breakfast really fast, or take your time and slowly chew each bite?
- After your delicious breakfast you get to do WHATEVER activity you would like to do. Keeping your thoughts to yourself for just right now...What activity do you choose? Is it something you can do outside, or will you do your activity inside? Is your activity something you do by yourself or with other people? If with other people, who will it be?
- After you have had SO MUCH FUN doing your activity, you are told you get to choose to go to your favorite place you like to go to. Keeping your thoughts to yourself for just right now...Where is your favorite place? How will you get there? Who will come with you?
- Keep your eyes closed for just a bit longer, and imagine you are just getting ready for bed after the most fun filled day ever! You are tired but still have a HUGE smile on your face.
- You climb into bed under warm covers with your favorite toy at your side and you are SO HAPPY as you think about the fun things you got to do...the people you played with... the delicious food you got to eat... and the good sleep you are about to have. You are happy and thankful for the great day. You can't wait to get up in the morning and do it all again.
- What parts of your day are you most happy and thankful for? What parts of your day are you most excited to do again tomorrow? Before you open your eyes, try to remember how good it feels at the end of the day to be happy about all the fun things you got to do during your day.
- Keep that feeling in mind, and very slowly open your eyes.

Closure

IN THE CLASSROOM

A/B Partner Talk, in partners children verbally describe the activities/food/things they like and are thankful for (each partner gets a turn). As a class, each child will share one thing their partner is thankful for. Class discussion about the different kinds of things everyone is grateful for, this will give children more ideas about the types of "every day" things we can give thanks for and feel grateful about.

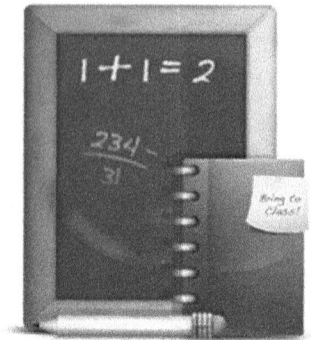

Assessment

Please see Page 61 in Activity Sheets Section for Rubric

FROM HOME

After reading through the exercise, ask the child to describe the kinds of activities/food/ things they like and are thankful for. To make the exercise more interactive, the parent/adult can also share the kinds of things they are grateful for. Then follow up with an age appropriate discussion about the different types of "every day" things we can give thanks for and feel grateful about.

Extension Idea

Have/help children write a "Journal Entry" and draw a picture of one or two things they are grateful for.

Activity #2 - Language Arts

BRAINSTORMING, MIND MAPPING SESSION

Lesson Objective/Outcome

For learners to start thinking about the different things in their lives they like and are thankful for. To write down six different things they are grateful for. To provide learners with a tool and reminder of the things they are grateful for.

Preparation and Resources

Page 21 from **Grateful Jake** is the hook and reference for this lesson.

See Page 49 & 50 in Activity Sheets for Brainstorming handout & reference of what a finished product may look like.

Lesson Idea

<u>Hook:</u> Read Grateful Jake.

Write the passage from page 21 on the board or overhead to act as a reference and a simple way of describing what 'being grateful' means. If doing this exercise from home, an option is to write the passage down on a paper or keep page 21 open for reference.

Passage from page 21:
*being grateful was feeling thankful
for the things he liked to do
that were fun and made him feel good.*

Each student receives a handout with a cloud in the center for brainstorming ideas.

IN THE CLASSROOM

Using the passage above as the hook, start the lesson as a class, brainstorm ideas of the different types of things we may feel grateful for on a daily basis to get learners started.

*Note: there is a teacher copy of this handout for your reference, it can be found in the activity sheets section.

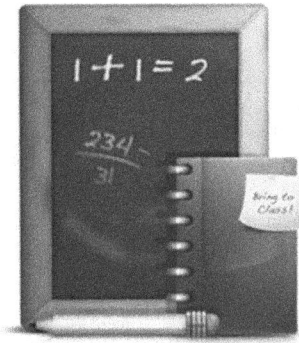

Students can then add six different things they are grateful for on their brainstorming handout individually or in pairs. If time allows, students can colour their mindmaps.

Display finished handouts on the bulletin board around the title:
THE GRATEFUL GRADE 2's

Closure

Class share the various ideas created in their own brainstorming session. Add a few of the answers to the Word Wall.

Extension Idea

Create a space/poster in the room called "Things We Are Grateful For". Over time, add different ideas to help students create more ideas of the things they too may be grateful for. This will also serve as a good refresher and reminder of what Gratitude and being Grateful means.

Assessment:

Please see Page 61 in Activity Sheets Section for Rubric

FROM HOME

Adult/caregiver will use the passage above to start a brainstorm session with the child. Together come up with ideas of the different kinds of things we may feel grateful for on a daily basis to get started.

*Note: there is a finished example of this handout for your reference, it can be found in the activity sheets section.

Child can then add six different things they are grateful for on their brainstorming handout with or without assistance (depending on their age). Then the child can colour their mind-map.

Display the finished handout in a prominent and visible place in the home to act as a daily reminder of the kinds of things the child is grateful for.

Closure

Parent/Caregiver could fill out their own handout and share their ideas with the child to make it more interactive and to show the child that everyone can be grateful no matter how young or old we may be.

Extension Idea

Create a "Family handout" where all members of the family share some of the things they are grateful for on one poster board and then display it in the family room or on the fridge and title it "The _____ Family is Grateful".

Activity #3 - Language Arts

GRATITUDE JOURNAL

Lesson Objective/Outcome

For learners to create a personal gratitude journal. The journal will be used to regularly add their thoughts and pictures of the people, places and things that they feel happy and grateful for. The gratitude journal helps learners develop more awareness of what makes them feel good. It also acts as a confidence booster and reminder of all the great things in their lives.

Preparation and Resources

1 Journal style Booklet, or blank sheets of paper that can be stapled together to make a booklet (See Activity Sheets for a template), pictures of family, friends etc. or symbolic pictures from magazines to make a personal title page (this could also be a drawing or artwork created by the child), pencil crayons, glue, stickers etc. Decorating the cover page can be done using a variety of materials and methods, it is ideal for children to create it in a way provides them with a sense of ownership.

See Page 51 in Activity Sheets for journal template.

Lesson Idea

This lesson would be best suited after Grateful Jake has been read, and after Activity #1 and #2 so the children will have been introduced to the concept of gratitude and will have had the opportunity to start thinking about things they are grateful for.

For an example of what a gratitude journal looks like visit the Cool Kids blog on www.emilymadill.com

IN THE CLASSROOM

Pick a regular day of the week, or daily if it works, and have the students add an entry in their Gratitude Journal. Monday mornings are great as the weekend is still fresh in their minds. Children write one or two things they are most grateful for that day or something they are grateful for from the weekend. Then they draw a corresponding picture above the journal entry. Creating this kind of ritual is a great way to set the tone for the day and is also a wonderful way for children to practice what being grateful feels like.

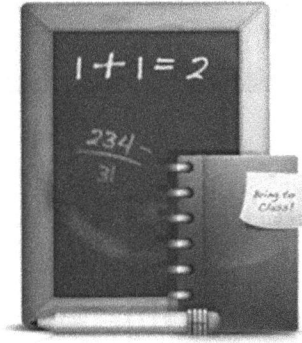

Closure

A/B Partner Talk where partners share their journal entry with each other. Regularly do a class share, so partners have an opportunity to share their entries with the whole class. An idea is to split the class up, Mondays could be group A's turn to share one thing from their Gratitude Journal and Fridays could be group B's turn.

Assessment

Please see Page 61 in Activity Sheets Section for Rubric.

FROM HOME

Set aside a special time for the child to add to their journal, whether it is each night before bed or at the end of every week. Creating this routine and ritual is an excellent opportunity for bonding and also for opening up discussions around gratitude. Depending on the age of the child, they could either write their own entry, or they could tell the parent/caregiver what to write for them, and then the child will draw a picture to represent the journal entry.

Closure

An excellent way to make this more interactive and meaningful is for the parent/caregiver to be there while the child is adding their entry. There is no age limit on the benefits of feeling grateful, so this is a perfect opportunity for the parent/caregiver to write in their own gratitude journal. Then the parent/caregiver shares their entry with the child to make it more interactive and powerful. This is a wonderful way for the parent/caregiver and child to do something together that is positive and uplifting.

Activity #4 - Language Arts/Art

GRATITUDE PLACEMAT

Lesson Objective/Outcome

To create a personal gratitude placemat the child will have as a keepsake and tool to remind them about the great things in their lives. The completed placemat acts as a regular confidence booster.

Preparation and Resources

Poster board or construction paper, placemat size (11 x 14), pencil crayons, felts, stickers and any material you wish to use for decorating. The last step is to have the placemats laminated to make them more durable, most stationary stores offer laminating services.

Lesson Idea

This lesson would be best suited after Grateful Jake has been read, and after Activity #1 and #2 so the children will have been introduced to the concept of gratitude and will have had the opportunity to start thinking about things they are grateful for.

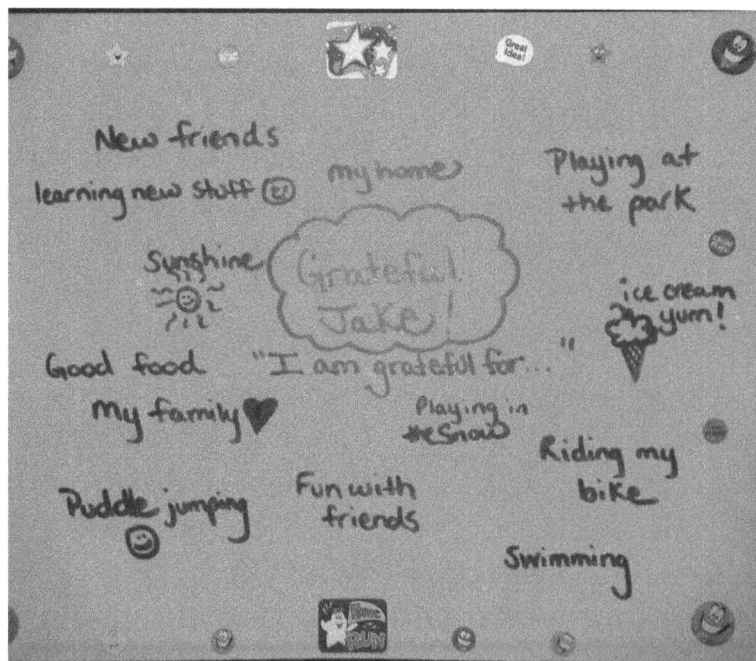

IN THE CLASSROOM

Students use the various ideas from their warm up exercise and brainstorming session to help them create a gratitude placemat. A great starting point is for them to write their name in the middle of the poster board, for example:

Jake's Gratitude Placemat
I Am Grateful for:

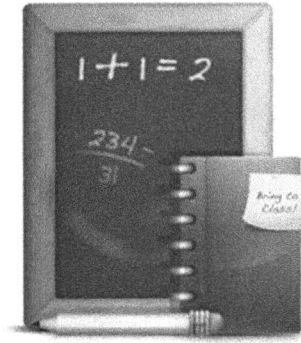

The point form descriptions/words of the things they are grateful for will be written around the placemat. They can also add colorful drawings, empowering stickers and decorations that will make it personal to them.

Closure

Have the placemats laminated to ensure they are durable. Each student will be given the opportunity to share their placemat with the class. Keep the placemats in the classroom and bring them out every day for students to use at snack time. This will provide a powerful and consistent reminder of what they are grateful for.

Extension Idea

Students make Gratitude placemats as a gift for their parents/caregivers at Christmas, Valentine's day, or Mother's/Father's day. Students would then add all of the things they are grateful for about the recipient (similar format as their own placemat).

Assessment

Please see Page 62 in Activity Sheets Section for Rubric.

FROM HOME

Children use the various ideas from their warm up exercise and brainstorming session to help them create a gratitude placemat. A great starting point is for them to write their name in the middle of the poster board, for example:

Jake's Gratitude Placemat
I Am Grateful for:

The point form descriptions/words of the things they are grateful for will be written around the placemat. They can also add colorful drawings, empowering stickers and decorations that will make it personal to them.

Note: If creating this activity with a younger child, the adult can brainstorm with the child and then write their ideas on the placemat. Then the child can decorate the placemat however they wish.

Closure

Have the placemat laminated to ensure it is durable. Bring the placemat out at every possible opportunity for the child to use (i.e. breakfast, lunch, dinner or snack time). It will help to instill a sense of pride and ownership, while also acting as a consistent reminder of what they are grateful for.

Extension Idea

Make Gratitude placemats as gifts for other members of the family (i.e. parents, siblings, grandparents, cousins, good friends, etc.) and add all of the things the child is grateful for about the recipient (similar format as their own placemat), Parents/caregivers could also make them for children.

Activity #5 - Performing Arts

A TRIP TO THE BEACH NARRATIVE PANTOMIME

Lesson Objective/Outcome
To use a variety of movements and expressions to practice feeling happy and grateful. To reinforce the notion that there are many regular everyday things we can feel grateful for.

Preparation and Resources
This lesson would be best suited after Grateful Jake has been read, and could either go before or after the other Activities.

Set up a clear safe space for children, ideal activity for the gymnasium. If doing this activity at home, it could be set up outdoors or wherever space allows.

Have a bell or chime of some kind to let the children know their cue to do their action.

See Page 52 in Activity Sheets for the Narrative Pantomime.

Lesson Idea
Before starting the exercise, give students an orientation on the setting of the narrative pantomime

IN THE CLASSROOM
Give children an opportunity to try out a few of the miming actions (e.g. happily jumped in the air with big arms). Remind them to be mindful of staying within their personal space and to use their bodies and not their words to communicate the various actions that will be given to them throughout the story (see activity sheets section page for the narrative pantomime).

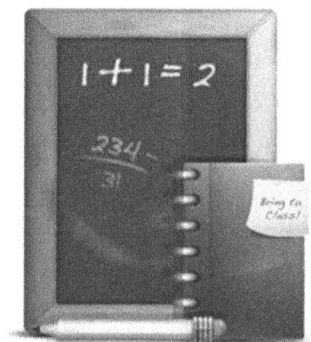

It's always great for the instructor to practice narrating the pantomime prior to using it with the class to see if there are any options to add light background music or sound effects.

Closure
Class Discussion.

Assessment
Please see Page 62 in Activity Sheets Section for Rubric.

FROM HOME
* A Narrative Pantomime is when someone narrates a story, the adult in this case (see activity sheets section page for the narrative pantomime) and the child "acts" out the action as stated by the narrator, using their body and not their words, much like a mime would.

Give children an opportunity to try out a few of the miming actions (e.g. happily jumped in the air with big arms). Remind them to use their bodies and not their words to communicate the various actions that will be given to them throughout the story. It's always great for the parent/caregiver to practice narrating the pantomime prior to using it to see if there are any options to add light background music or sound effects.

Closure
Have an open discussion with the child or as a family.

Extension Idea
Topic of discussion: discuss the different types of feelings Jake had during his trip to the beach, i.e. happy, patient (calm) etc. and why he felt grateful at the end of the day. Also talk about how regular things, like having fun playing with friends/family or enjoying a delicious, healthy lunch are regular things we can practice feeling grateful for.

Activity #6 - Nature Walk

GRATITUDE ROCK NATURE WALK

Lesson Objective/Outcome

To get children outside, moving their bodies and connecting with nature. For children to select a rock they find on their journey to have as a keepsake and reminder of the importance of getting outside and enjoying the natural beauty accessible to everyone.

Preparation and Resources

Find a safe nature trail, beach trail, or some kind of walkway for an outing/fieldtrip. Select an area where children will have a number of examples of nature (i.e. trees, plants, birds etc). Also keep in mind to choose somewhere they can select a rock to bring home with them (preferably something small they can paint/decorate). Art supplies such as paint, felts stickers, etc. to decorate their rock.

Lesson Idea

HOOK: Read Grateful Jake and complete a few of the previous activities so children are more grounded in what being grateful means and feels like. This will also help give them a reference to better understand that we can be grateful for some of the simpler things in life that are free.

IN THE CLASSROOM

Prepare students for the nature walk and let them know they will be selecting a rock of their choice to become their Gratitude Rock. They will then get to decorate their rock to have as a keepsake. Their Gratitude Rock will help remind them of the importance of getting outside to play and to feel grateful for the simple things in life that are free for everyone (like playing outside or at the park, enjoying fresh air, going for a walk, playing tag with friends etc).

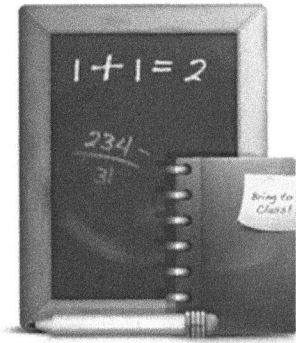

Extension Idea

Class Brainstorm Session some of the different things we can do that won't cost money and are still fun and enjoyable to do. This will help set the tone that there are many things we can do that are free, fun and healthy!

Closure

A/B Partner share using their Gratitude Rocks, students will share why their rock is meaningful to them with their partner. Then students will participate in a class share where children have the opportunity to share one thing their Gratitude Rock Means to them with the entire class. Create a Class Gratitude Rock display to showcase their decorated rocks before they take them home.

Extension Idea

Create a "Classroom Gratitude Rock" that could be used on Monday mornings to create a ritual where each member of the class gets a turn to hold the rock and share one thing that happened during their weekend they are grateful for.

Assessment

Please see Page 62 in Activity Sheets Section for Rubric.

FROM HOME

Prepare children for the nature walk and let them know they will be selecting a rock of their choice to become their Gratitude Rock. They will then get to decorate their rock to have as a keepsake. Their Gratitude Rock will help remind them of the importance of getting outside to play and to feel grateful for the simple things in life that are free for everyone (like playing outside or at the park, enjoying fresh air, going for a walk, playing tag with friends etc).

Extension Idea

Discuss as a family some of the different things we can do that won't cost money and are still fun and enjoyable to do. This will help set the tone that there are many things we can do that are free, fun and healthy.

Closure

Have a discussion with the child so they can share what their Gratitude Rock means to them. Create a special place in their room or in the home where they can display their rock.

Extension Idea

Create a "Family Gratitude Rock" that could be used at dinner time, bedtime or to create a ritual where each member of the family gets a turn to hold the rock and share one thing that happened in their day they are grateful for.

Activity #7 - Art

I AM GRATEFUL FOR ME SELF PORTRAIT

Lesson Objective/Outcome

For children to create a 'life size' drawing of themselves as a symbol of their uniqueness and greatness. After tracing an outline of their bodies they will draw their body parts they are grateful to have, e.g. eyes for seeing, nose for smelling, mouth for eating etc. The main objective is for children to begin creating awareness and gratitude for their health and their bodies. This would be a great activity for promoting healthy body image or as a fun science project.

Preparation and Resources

Large rolls of art paper that would be suitable for children to trace silhouettes of themselves. Scissors for cutting out their silhouettes. Pencils/Pencil Crayons/Felts for drawing their self portrait and different body parts on their life size outline.

Lesson Idea

HOOK: Read Grateful Jake. Have a discussion around the idea we are all unique and how each of us 'look' on the outside is a special way we can tell each other part. An idea is to also discuss how we can feel thankful for our differences and that not everyone has body parts that will work in the same way as others and that we can feel grateful for the parts of our bodies that do work well and are healthy.

IN THE CLASSROOM

Teacher will help students create outlines of the silhouettes (best done with child lying flat on the art paper). After outline is drawn, student/teacher will use scissors to cut around the outline. Students will complete their self-portraits using coloured pencils/felts to draw in their body parts they are grateful for.

Closure

Each student has the opportunity to share their finished silhouette with the class.

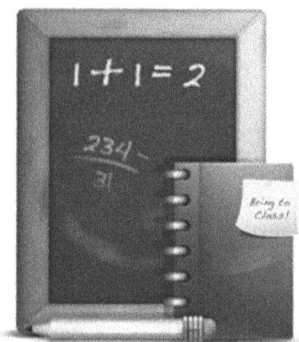

Extension Idea

Display Student's outlines around the room or in an area with a title: "We are Proud to be Strong and Healthy" or "We are Grateful for our Bodies".

Assessment

Please see Page 63 in Activity Sheets Section for Rubric.

FROM HOME

Parent/caregiver will help child create an outline of their silhouette (best done with child lying flat on the art paper). After outline is drawn, adult/child (age dependent) use scissors to cut outline. Child uses coloured pencils/felts to draw in their body parts they are grateful for.

Closure

Display child's outline in a special place, e.g. playroom, family room etc.

Extension Idea

Create silhouettes for each member of the family and display in a special place in the home.

Activity #8 - Confidence Booster

GRATITUDE/LIKE BOX

Lesson Objective/Outcome
Children will create a gratitude box to store special words written about the things they like about themselves and the confident boosting things their friends and family have written about them.

Preparation and Resources
Old shoe box, Kleenex box, cereal box etc. that will be decorated for child to use as their Gratitude/Like Box. Some ideas for decorating include: covering the box in wrapping paper of the child's choice, wrapping the box in regular paper and then using felt pens, pencil crayons etc. to decorate the paper, create a picture collage by gluing photos onto the box that are special to the child (i.e. family photos), or pictures from a magazine.

Pencil/pen for filling out the written confident boosters that go in the box (see activity sheets section for the template). Some of the strips of paper will say: "What I Like About Me", "A Great thing in my life is", "What I Like About You", "I Like That You" (the first two are intended for the child to fill out about themselves, and the last two are for parent/caregiver/teacher/family/ friend etc. to fill out about the child).

**This is an ongoing activity that the child, teacher, parent/caregiver, family and friends can add to over time. It serves as a confident booster every time something new is added, and every time the child reads the compliments already in their box.

See Page 53 in Activity Sheets for 'Confident booster template'.

Lesson Idea
Before starting this activity, it is ideal to complete the previous activities so children will have already had the opportunity to think about what they are grateful for in their own lives.

IN THE CLASSROOM

Students will spend time decorating their special gratitude box that is just for them. Ensure there is a lid or opening in the box so they can easily access their compliments whenever they want.

Students will fill out a strip of paper that says "What I like About Me" and "A Great thing in my life is" to get the box started (see handout in activity sheets section for the template).

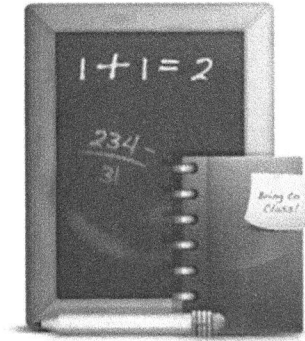

The teacher will add two compliments to each student's gratitude box, i.e. "What I Like About You" and "I Like that You" to help get the box started.

Extension Idea

Create a ritual where students are given the opportunity to add to their gratitude box and to another student's box. By the end of the year, each student will have one compliment from each of their classmates as well as a number of positive things they have written about themselves.

Closure

Children keep their boxes in a special place where they can access them to add new compliments to. They can bring their box out whenever they need a little boost to feel good about themselves.

FROM HOME

Children will spend time decorating their special gratitude box that is just for them. Ensure there is a lid or opening in the box so they can easily access their compliments whenever they want.

Children will fill out a strip of paper that says "What I like About Me" and "A Great thing in my life is" to get the box started (see handout in activity sheets section for the template).

The parent/caregiver will add two compliments to the child's gratitude box, i.e. "What I Like About You" and "I Like that You" to help get the box started.

Closure

Children keep their boxes in a special place where they can access them to add new compliments to. They can bring their box out whenever they need a little boost to feel good about themselves, or whenever special visitors come who will add more compliments.

Extension Idea

Parents/Caregivers can also create their own gratitude/like boxes and have other members of the family add to their boxes as well. It is great for children to see that we are never too young or old to practice feeling good about ourselves or to pay a compliment to someone else.

Activity #9 - Confidence Booster

GIFTS OF CONFIDENCE

Lesson Objective/Outcome

For children to practice sharing their appreciation and gratitude for other people in their lives. For children to also practice receiving appreciation and compliments from other people.

"When we appreciate what someone does for us and share with that person why we are grateful, we give a gift of confidence to them and to ourselves." ~ Emily Madill

Preparation and Resources

See Page 54 in Activity Sheets for The Gift of Confidence handout.

Lesson Idea

IN THE CLASSROOM

Students fill out the Gift of Confidence handout by sharing why they are grateful for a 'selected' person in their life. The teacher will pair students so each student fills out a gift of confidence for their partner and each student receives a gift of confidence from their partner.

Extension Idea

The student could fill out a gift of confidence for a parent/caregiver or friend. The teacher could also fill out a gift of confidence for each student in the class.

Closure

Class discussion, discuss how it felt to 'receive' the gift of confidence and how it felt to 'give' the gift of confidence.

Extension Idea

Mount the Gift of Confidence on coloured construction paper and then laminate so the student could use it as a placemat for snack time or for when they are doing art at their desk. Bring the placemats out regularly as a great reminder and confidence booster.

FROM HOME

Children will fill out the Gift of Confidence handout by sharing why they are grateful for a 'selected' person in their life (eg. parent/caregiver or friend). The parent/caregiver will also fill out a gift of confidence for the child so the child has the opportunity to receive a gift of confidence as well as give one.

Closure

Discuss how it felt to 'receive' the gift of confidence and how it felt to 'give' the gift of confidence.

Extension Idea

Mount the Gift of Confidence on coloured construction paper and then laminate to use as a placemat for meal time or for when they are doing art. Bring the placemat out regularly as a great reminder and confidence booster.

GRATITUDE CARDS

Lesson Objective/Outcome

For children to practice expressing their appreciation and gratitude to people in their lives they care about. To have the opportunity to experience what it feels like to make someone else feel good by expressing their gratitude.

Preparation and Resources

See Page 55 in Activity Sheets for the Appreciation card template.

This works great on card stock or thicker paper, standard paper could also be used. Pen/pencil, pencil crayons/felts, anything to decorate the card to make it special.

Lesson Idea

IN THE CLASSROOM

Students will each create a Gratitude card for a loved one.

The card will include:

- A cover, that says 'Thank You for being YOU' with a space to write To: and From: and to draw a picture that represents the person they are grateful for.
- A Page where they can write some of the things they are thankful they get to do with the recipient.
- A Page where they can write about the things they like about the recipient.
- A page where they can write about why they are grateful to have the recipient in their life.
- Students will fold the handout along the dotted line to make it into a card.

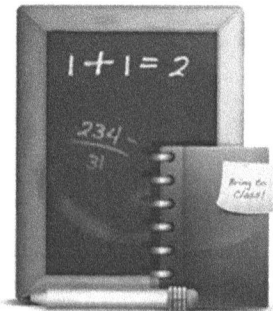

Closure

Discuss how it felt to 'give' the gratitude card to someone they care about and how that person reacted when they received the card from the child.

Assessment

Please see Page 63 in Activity Sheets Section for Rubric.

FROM HOME

Child will create a Gratitude card for a loved one.

The card will include:

- A cover, that says 'Thank You for being YOU' with a space to write To: and From: and to draw a picture that represents the person they are grateful for.
- A Page where they can write some of the things they are thankful they get to do with the recipient.
- A Page where they can write about the things they like about the recipient.
- A page where they can write about why they are grateful to have the recipient in their life.
- Children will fold the handout along the dotted line to make it into a card.

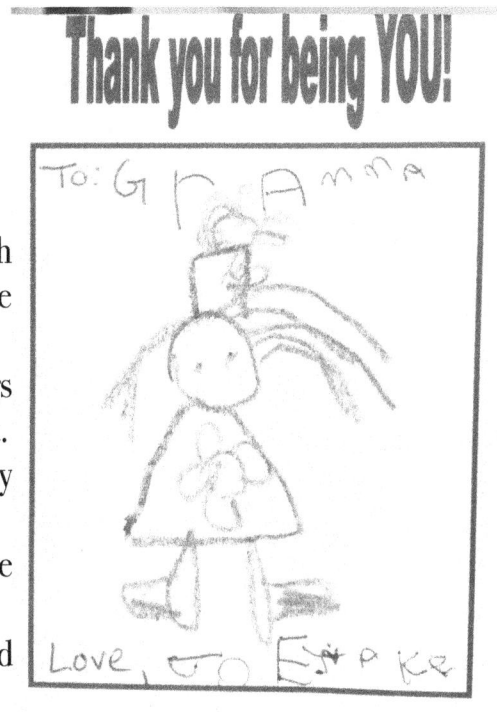

Closure

Discuss how it felt to 'give' the gratitude card to someone they care about and how that person reacted when they received the card from the child.

Activity #11 - Confidence Booster

PAY IT FORWARD GIFT BOX

"Sometimes a small thing you do can mean everything in another person's life."
-Author Unknown

Lesson Objective/Outcome

For children to experience the 'gift of giving' and help others in need. To help build compassion and empathy for others through the act of giving and to feel good about themselves in the process.

Preparation and Resources

The idea of this activity is for children to put together a gift box to give to someone in need. You could either choose an organization (local or abroad) or a family in need to be the recipient. It is great to pick a theme for the gifts that go in the box, i.e. it could be things to do outside, e.g. of items: skipping rope, beach towel, buckets and shovels, chalk, beach ball, etc.

The items should be age-appropriate and personalized for the recipient. Children will know ahead of time what organization or age of child the box is for and each child will be responsible for giving one item. It could also be something hand made by the child to give if budget is a concern, or the children could take part in fundraising to raise funds for the gift box.

There is flexibility in this activity to be innovative and to create lasting meaning for children. It is ideal for children to take part in the discussion process to understand why they are giving to the person/organization in need. This will help them feel more ownership and connection to the act of giving.

This is a great class activity that could be extended into a school wide project. If you are doing this from home, it is great to get everyone in the family involved and if possible to get other families to take part. It would be ideal to start this project before Christmas and have it ready to give around the Christmas season as a reminder to children that it feels good to 'give' to others.

Lesson Idea

IN THE CLASSROOM

Class discussion on how it feels when we give something to someone else that makes a difference in their lives, even if it is a small difference. Give some background on the recipient of the gift box (if it is for a child or organization abroad it's a great opportunity to introduce a new country/culture to the children). Brainstorm session where the entire class takes part in choosing the theme for the gift box.

Closure

Have a discussion about how it felt to make a difference in the life of someone else. Discuss ways we can make a difference in the lives of others on a daily basis (e.g. through acts of kindness, saving pennies to give to local soup kitchens etc.)

Extension Idea

Designate a day/week to be 'Random Acts of Kindness' Day/Week. This is an excellent activity to do as a school wide initiative. Children and teachers will consciously take part in doing a random act of kindness each day for someone without any expectation of anything in return. The acts of kindness could be a smile, a note, a gift of confidence, helping someone in need or any number of things. It doesn't have to be something that is purchased. At the beginning of each day, children will have the opportunity to report their random act of kindness (RAK) from the previous day and how the recipient reacted, and how it made them feel to give without expectation. You could also create a class chart for recording students' RAK on.

FROM HOME

Have a family discussion about how it feels when we give something to someone else that makes a difference in their lives, even if it is a small difference. Give some background on the recipient of the gift box (if it is for a child or organization abroad it's a great opportunity to introduce a new country/culture). Everyone in the family will take part in choosing the theme for the gift box.

Closure

Have a discussion about how it felt to make a difference in the life of someone else. Discuss ways we can make a difference in the lives of others on a daily basis (e.g. through acts of kindness, saving pennies to give to local soup kitchens etc.)

Extension Idea

Designate a day/week to be 'Random Acts of Kindness' Day/Week in the household. Each day children and their caregivers will set the intention to consciously take part in doing a random act of kindness each day for someone without expectation of anything in return. The acts of kindness could be a smile, a note, a gift of confidence, helping someone in need or any number of things. It doesn't have to be something that is purchased. Depending on the age of the child, this is something the parent and child could set out to do together, or the child could be responsible for performing their own RAK during the day. Choose a time each day to discuss and record the RAK that each family member made during the day. You could also create a family chart for recording RAK made by family members.

Activity #12 - Language Arts

WHAT I HAVE LEARNED ABOUT GRATITUDE MINI-BOOK

Lesson Objective/Outcome

For children to create a summary of their learning around gratitude and being grateful. This is an excellent opportunity to create evidence of their learning. It is also a great chance for children to boost their confidence by creating a keepsake and reminder of what they are truly grateful for.

Preparation and Resources

See Page 56 in Activity Sheets for the Gratitude Mini-Book Template.

Lesson Idea

IN THE CLASSROOM

Students will create their own Gratitude Mini-Book to summarize their learning and to have a positive reminder on gratitude they will keep

The book will include:

- A cover, where they can add their name and a space to draw a picture that represents something they are grateful for, or a self-portrait where they are feeling happy and grateful.
- A Page where they can write some of the 'things' they are 'most grateful for'.
- A Page where they can write about some of the 'people' they are 'grateful to have in their life'.
- A page where they can write about some of the 'places' they are 'most grateful to go'.
- Students will use scissors to cut along the dotted lines. The books should be stapled after students have filled in their information and completed the front cover (with colour). Option: Instead of cutting the handout to make a book, students could fold the handout along the dotted line to make a card style book.

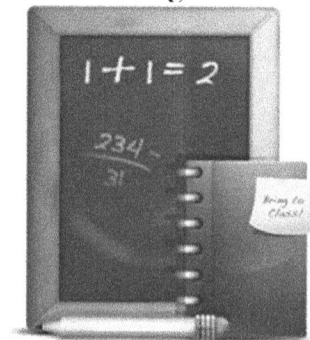

Closure

Give students the opportunity to share their books with the class or with a partner.

Extension Idea

Create a space for students to display their books, for example in the classroom reading area or library.

Assessment

Please see Page 63 in Activity Sheets Section for Rubric.

FROM HOME

Children and their caregivers will create their own Gratitude Mini-Book to summarize their learning and to have a positive reminder on gratitude they will keep.

The book will include:
- A cover, where they can add their name and a space to draw a picture that represents something they are grateful for, or a self-portrait where they are feeling happy and grateful.
- A Page where they can write some of the 'things' they are 'most grateful for'.
- A Page where they can write about some of the 'people' they are 'grateful to have in their life'.
- A page where they can write about some of the 'places' they are 'most grateful to go'.
- If age-appropriate, children can use scissors to cut along the dotted line. The books should be stapled after the children have filled in their information and completed the front cover (with colour). Option: Instead of cutting the handout to make a book, children could fold the handout along hte dotted line to make a card-style book.

Closure

Give children the opportunity to share their books with other family members and friends.

Extension Idea

Create a special place for children to display their books, for example in a family room or on a bookshelf.

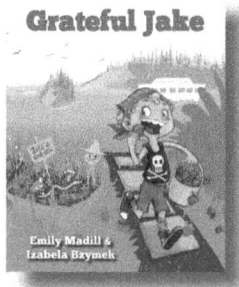

ACTIVITY SHEETS FOR GRATEFUL JAKE

Grateful: _____

Comprehension

1) What delicious berry did Jake love to eat from his garden box?

2) At the end of the story why did Jake get up from the dinner table and run to his room in a hurry?

3) Jake said being grateful was feeling _____ for the things he liked to do that were fun and made him feel good.

Word Study

Please write these words in alphabetical order:

sleep	happy	wash	found	bike

Add the suffixes "**s**" and "**ing**" to the end of these words:

a) sleep   b) feel   c) play   d) read   e) thank

Something to think about:

If you had to do the same homework assignment as Jake, what 10 things would **YOU** write down that **YOU** are grateful for?

Grateful Jake Story Sequence

Beginning   **Middle**   **End**

In the Beginning: In the Middle: In the End:

Grateful Jake Story Sequence (Adapted Version)

Beginning	**Middle**	**End**

In the Beginning:	In the Middle:	In the End:

Warm Up Exercise

- Close your eyes and imagine you are just waking up in the morning from a long, comfortable sleep.

- You stretch your arms high above your head as you let out a long yawn.

- Look around your bedroom, what do you see? Do you have some favorite toys or things that are just for you that you keep in your room?

- Keeping your thoughts to yourself for just right now… Pick up one of your favorite toys and bring it with you as you walk to your kitchen where your breakfast is ready, waiting for you to enjoy.

- Keeping your eyes closed for now, think of how happy you feel to see your favorite breakfast. What does your breakfast look like? What does it taste like? Do you eat your breakfast really fast, or take your time and slowly chew each bite?

- After your delicious breakfast you get to do WHATEVER activity you would like to do.

- Keeping your thoughts to yourself for just right now…What activity do you choose? Is it something you can do outside, or will you do your activity inside? Is your activity something you do by yourself or with other people? If with other people, who will it be?

- After you have had SO MUCH FUN doing your activity, you are told you get to choose to go to your favorite place you like to go to.

- Keeping your thoughts to yourself for just right now…Where is your favorite place? How will you get there? Who will come with you?

- Keep your eyes closed for just a bit longer, and imagine you are just getting ready for bed after the most fun filled day ever! You are tired but still have a HUGE smile on your face.

- You climb into bed under warm covers with your favorite toy at your side and you are SO HAPPY as you think about the fun things you got to do…the people you played with…the delicious food you got to eat… and the good sleep you are about to have.

- You are happy and thankful for the great day. You can't wait to get up in the morning and do it all again.

- What parts of your day are you most happy and thankful for? What parts of your day are you most excited to do again tomorrow? Before you open your eyes, try to remember how good it feels at the end of the day to be happy about all the fun things you got to do during your day.

- Keep that feeling in mind, and very slowly open your eyes.

Let's Brainstorm

I AM GRATEFUL

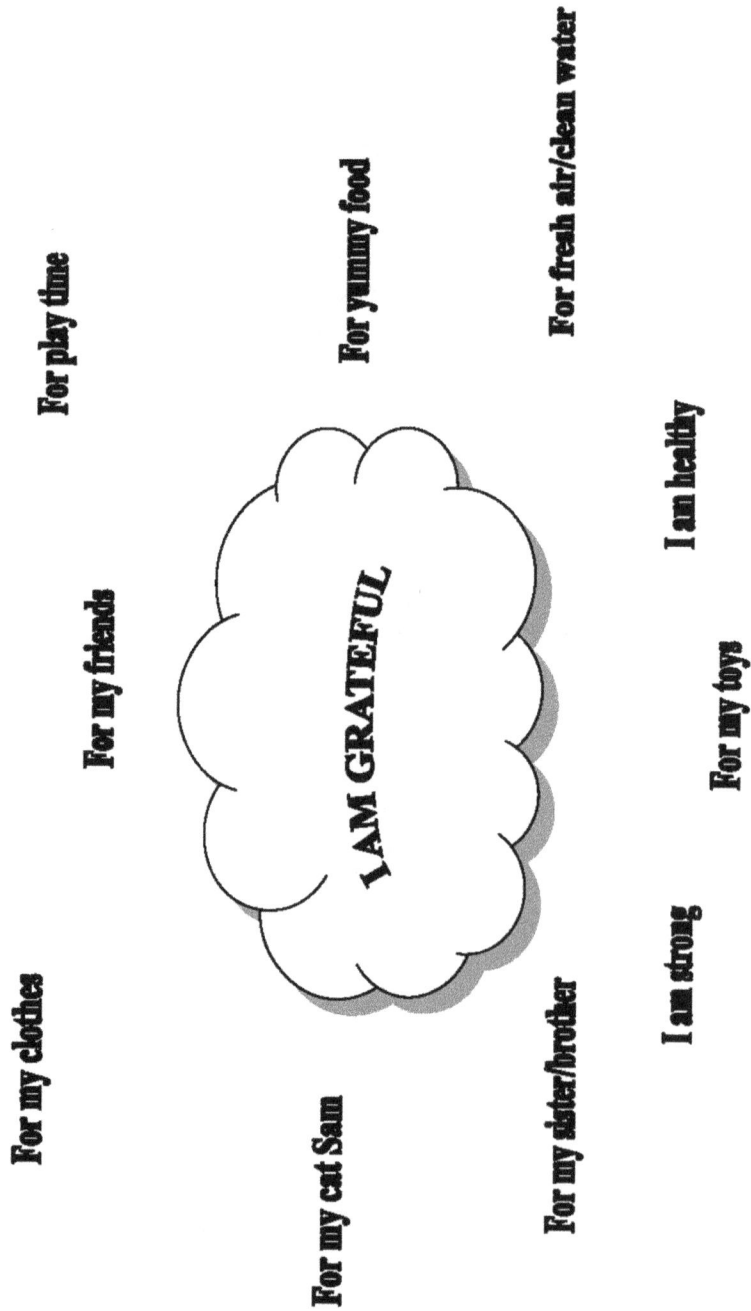

For fresh air/clean water

For yummy food

For play time

I am healthy

For my friends

I AM GRATEFUL

For my toys

For my clothes

I am strong

For my cat Sam

For my sister/brother

I am Grateful for:

_____

_____

_____

_____

Narrative Pantomime:

*Reminder at the beginning: As I am reading this narrative pantomime, *A Trip to the Beach* aloud remember you are using your bodies and not your voices to show what you are thinking and feeling. Please keep your hands to yourself and stay in your personal space while you are acting out the pantomime. Every time you hear this sound (*Have a bell or chime of some kind to let the children know their cue to do their action) you will know it's time to do your action. ****Note: Underlined text represents the action students will mime. The "Pause" is there to give players enough time to mime the action.**

A Trip to the Beach…

It was a warm summer morning and the perfect kind of day for a trip to the beach. Jake quickly grabbed his backpack and **EXCITEDLEY stuffed it full with all his favorite things he would need** for a day at the beach (PAUSE). Jake's Mom let him know his cousins, Samantha, Taylor and Colton would also be joining them for a picnic lunch at the beach. "Yahoo!" Jake exclaimed, as he **HAPPILY jumped in the air with big arms** (PAUSE). He loved going to the beach with his family and enjoyed it even more when he got the chance to play with his cousins. He felt so grateful, and as he thought about all the fun he was going to have Jake **wore a giant GRIN from ear to ear** (PAUSE).

Jake and his brother Joe hopped in the car loaded with a delicious picnic lunch, buckets, shovels, kites and more! As soon as they pulled up, he raced to the beach, kicked off his shoes and went right into the water. Jake loved how the cool water felt as **he had FUN hopping over the small waves that splashed up on the shore** (PAUSE).
Jake spotted his cousins building a gigantic sandcastle, so he ran over to join in the fun. He took his shovel **and EAGERLY joined the others to dig a deep moat around the castle** (PAUSE).

Jake's Mom called them for lunch. Samantha, Taylor, Joe, Jake & Colton all shouted "Yippee!" at the same time as they raced to the picnic table. The kids all enjoyed juicy watermelon and fresh strawberries. Samantha and Jake **SAVOURED their yummy homemade chocolate chip cookies one delicious bite at a time** (PAUSE).
Jake had enough healthy and tasty food to eat and took one last long sip of his water. The next part of their plan was flying kites, and they were in luck because the wind had just started to pick up. Jake **unreeled the kite string by PATIENTLY winding the handle nice and slow** (PAUSE). A gust of wind blew and his green dragon kite lifted up to soar effortlessly in the sky. He **HAPPILY held onto the handle as he steered the kite to make it dip up and down and go side to side** (PAUSE).

After flying kites and another swim in the lake, the day had come to an end. Jake said goodbye to all of his cousins and then raced Joe to the car. On the drive home, Jake **looked out of the window with a BIG SMILE on his face as he thought of the fun day** (PAUSE). He was trying to figure out what part of the day he enjoyed the most and then decided it was the whole day he was grateful for. Jake's Mom asked the boys if they had a good day, and at the same time they both said "We had the BEST day!" "Can we do it AGAIN tomorrow?" ~ THE END

Gratitude Box Confidence Booster

What I Like About Me:	What I Like About Me:
What I Like About You:	What I Like About You:
A Great thing in my life is:	A Great thing in my life is:
I Like That You:	I Like That You:
What I Like About Me:	What I Like About Me:
What I Like About You:	What I Like About You:
A Great thing in my life is:	A Great thing in my life is:
I Like That You:	I Like That You:
What I Like About Me:	What I Like About Me:
What I Like About You:	What I Like About You:
A Great thing in my life is:	A Great thing in my life is:
I Like That You:	I Like That You:

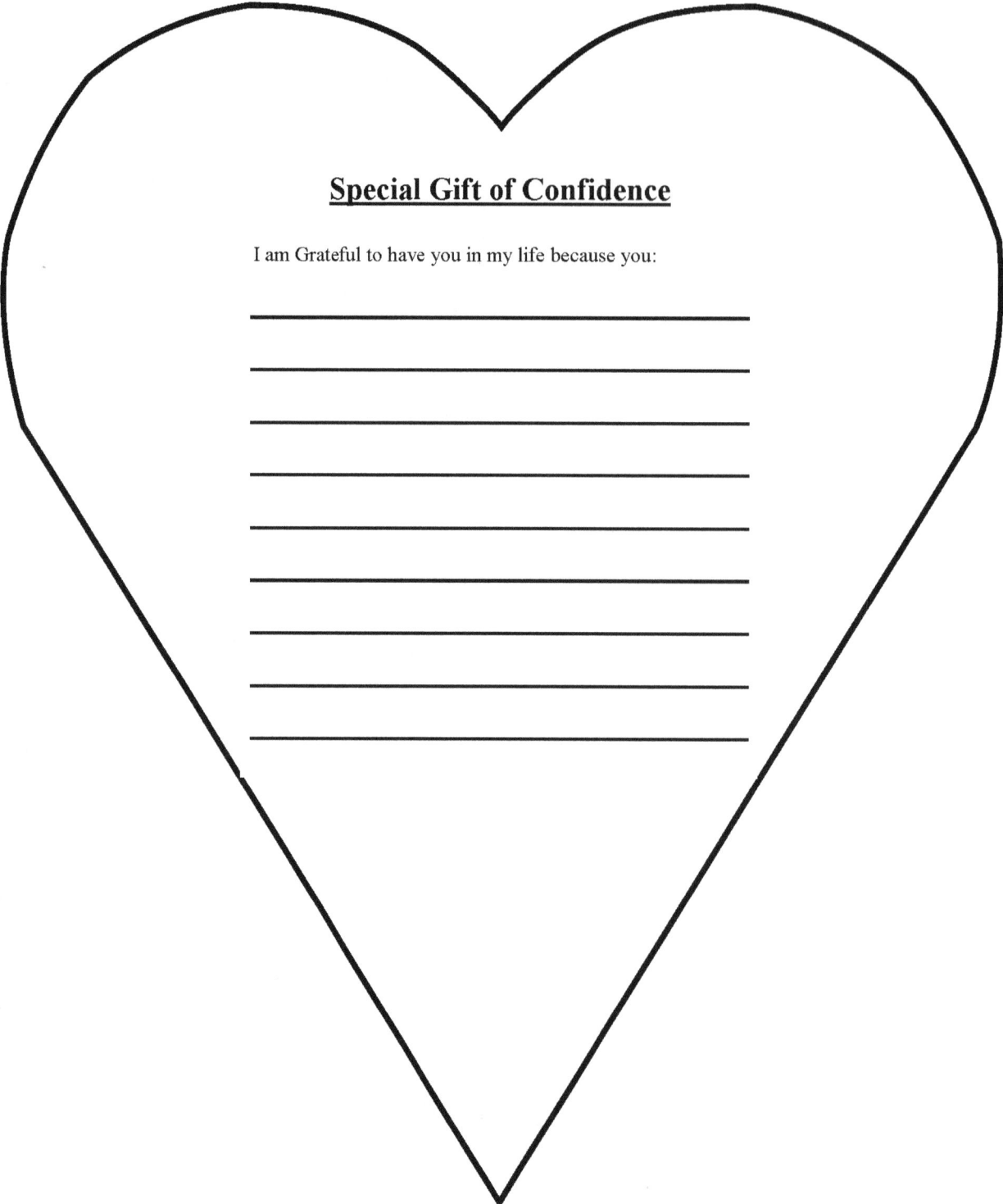

Special Gift of Confidence

I am Grateful to have you in my life because you:

_____

_____

_____

_____

_____

_____

_____

_____

_____

Thank you for being YOU!

I am grateful to have you
in my life because you:

I am thankful that we get to
do these things together:

I appreciate these things
about you:

GRATEFUL!

"Being Grateful means feeling thankful for the things I like that are fun and make me feel good."

Some of the things I am most grateful for are:

_____
_____
_____
_____
_____

Some of the people I am grateful to have in my life are:

_____
_____
_____
_____
_____

Some of the places I am most grateful to go are:

_____
_____
_____
_____
_____
_____
_____
_____

Vocabulary for spelling tests

bike	lake
found	play
game	read
gave	swim
grateful	thankful
happy	wash

* **Please note**: The above words are intended to be used, one or two at a time, as an addition to weekly spelling tests or as an addition to the Word Wall. The words range in difficulty level from moderate to more complicated.

Mathematics

Add the numbers in each box to discover what the message below says.

A 5 7 + 1 --------------	E 8 3 + 3 --------------	F 5 3 + 1 --------------	G 9 3 + 3 --------------
H 9 5 + 2 --------------	I 5 3 + 2 --------------	L 1 2 + 3 --------------	R 4 2 + 5 --------------
	T 7 3 + 2 --------------	V 1 2 + 1 --------------	

‾‾‾‾‾‾‾   ‾‾‾‾‾‾‾ ‾‾‾‾‾‾‾   ‾‾‾‾‾‾‾ ‾‾‾‾‾‾‾   ‾‾‾‾‾‾‾
  10   16   13   4   14   13

    ‾‾‾‾‾‾‾ ‾‾‾‾‾‾‾   ‾‾‾‾‾‾‾ ‾‾‾‾‾‾‾ ‾‾‾‾‾‾‾
     15   11   14   13   12

      ‾‾‾‾‾ ‾‾‾‾‾‾‾ ‾‾‾‾‾‾ ‾‾‾‾‾‾ !
       6   10   9   14

Add the numbers in each box to discover what the message below says.

A	E	F	G
5 7 + 1 ----------- **13**	8 3 + 3 ----------- **14**	5 3 + 1 ----------- **9**	9 3 + 3 ----------- **15**
H 9 5 + 2 ----------- **16**	**I** 5 3 + 2 ----------- **10**	**L** 1 2 + 3 ----------- **6**	**R** 4 2 + 5 ----------- **11**
	T 7 3 + 2 ----------- **12**	**V** 1 2 + 1 ----------- **4**	

I HAVE A
GREAT LIFE!

Grateful Jake Word Search

```
E   K   I   B   R   S   Q   J   G   K   T
Q   K   J   E   S   W   K   P   A   W   C
R   L   A   E   H   X   Q   C   M   Y   R
E   D   U   M   O   K   X   S   E   P   S
A   K   I   F   S   I   U   D   Y   P   O
J   W   A   P   E   N   Y   A   S   A   Z
S   A   G   L   W   T   L   D   A   H   F
D   F   K   X   I   P   A   R   Z   I   U
E   G   I   E   H   E   D   R   A   T   H
I   Z   M   Z   X   I   V   Y   G   C   Y
F   J   Z   L   U   F   K   N   A   H   T
```

bike	Jake
car	lake
game	play
grateful	read
happy	swim
hose	thankful

Assessment Rubrics

Outcome	Criteria				Total
	1 (Not yet)	2 (Meets)	3 (Fully Meets)	4 (Exceeds)	
Demonstrate good listening skills during teacher reading of "Warm up Exercise"	Did not listen or stay on task at all during the warm up exercise	Listened for some of the warm up exercise, but not all	Listened without speaking for the entire warm up exercise	Listened, kept eyes closed and appeared relaxed for the entire reading of the warm up exercise	
Demonstrate good listening skills during A/B Partner Talk	Unwilling to participate in A/B Partner talk	Willing to take turns listening, but interrupted or spoke out of turn	Listened without speaking while partner shared	Listened without speaking while partner shared and also paraphrased something back to partner that he/she shared	
Demonstrate good reporting out skills during class share	Did not remember anything that partner was thankful for or was unwilling to participate in class share	Remembered one thing that partner was thankful for, but did not speak clearly or make eye contact with the audience	Remembered one thing that partner was thankful for, spoke clearly and made eye contact with the audience	Remembered one thing that partner was thankful for, spoke clearly, made eye contact with the audience and asked if anyone had any questions	

Assessment, Activity #2

Outcome	Criteria				Total
	1 (Not yet)	2 (Meets)	3 (Fully Meets)	4 (Exceeds)	
Create a mindmap with 6 different things they are grateful for	Did not brainstorm any thoughts for mindmap	Had 3 or more things they're thankful for written down on mindmap	Had at least 6 things they're grateful for written down on mindmap	Had 6 or more things they're grateful for written down on mindmap and added colour	
Work cooperatively with partner	Was unwilling to work with partner or share ideas	Worked cooperatively and stayed on task some of the time, shared some ideas	Worked cooperatively, was willing to share ideas and stayed on task	Worked cooperatively, was willing to share ideas, stayed on task, and gave praise to each other for ideas or finished mindmap	

Assessment, Activity #3

Outcome	Criteria				Total
	1 (Not yet)	2 (Meets)	3 (Fully Meets)	4 (Exceeds)	
Create Cover Page for personal Gratitude Journal	Left Page blank	Wrote their name to indicate it's their journal.	Wrote their name to indicate it's their journal and used one art element to decorate/personalize their journal.	Wrote their name to indicate it's their journal and used more than one art element to decorate/personalize their journal.	
Make 1st journal entry and draw a corresponding picture in personal Gratitude Journal	Left entire page blank	Wrote one thing they are grateful for.	Wrote one thing they are grateful for and drew a picture to represent their journal entry.	Wrote one or more things they are grateful for and drew a picture using one or more art elements to represent their journal entry.	

Assessment, Activity #4

Outcome	Criteria				Total
	1 (Not yet)	2 (Meets)	3 (Fully Meets)	4 (Exceeds)	
Write their names in the middle of Gratitude Placemat and add at least 6 things they are grateful for, personalize with one art element	Left the placemat blank	Wrote their name and at least 6 things they are grateful for.	Wrote their name, at least 6 things they are grateful for and added one art element to personalize the placemat	Wrote their name. 6 or more things they are grateful for and added more than one art element to personalize the placemat	
Demonstrated good speaking/presenting skills during class share of placemat.	Was unwilling to participate in presenting placemat	Willing to participate in presenting, could speak clearer and did not make eye contact with the audience	Willing to participate in presenting, spoke clearly and made eye contact.	Willing to participate in presenting, spoke clearly, made eye contact and asked the audience if anyone had questions.	

Assessment, Activity #5

Outcome	Criteria				Total
	1 (Not yet)	2 (Meets)	3 (Fully Meets)	4 (Exceeds)	
Demonstrate a willingness to participate in narrative pantomime and stayed on task for entire exercise	Was not willing to participate in narrative pantomime	Was willing to participate in narrative pantomime and stayed on task for most of the exercise	Was willing to participate in narrative pantomime and stayed on task for the entire exercise	Was willing to participate in narrative pantomime stayed on task for the entire exercise and contributed to class discussion after the exercise	

Assessment, Activity #6

Outcome	Criteria				Total
	1 (Not yet)	2 (Meets)	3 (Fully Meets)	4 (Exceeds)	
Demonstrate good listening skills during A/B Partner Share of Gratitude Rock	Unwilling to participate in A/B Partner talk	Willing to take turns listening, but interrupted or spoke out of turn	Listened without speaking while partner shared	Listened without speaking while partner shared and also paraphrased something back to partner that he/she shared	

Assessment, Activity #7

Outcome	Criteria				Total
	1 (Not yet)	2 (Meets)	3 (Fully Meets)	4 (Exceeds)	
Demonstrate good speaking/presenting skills during class share of finished self-portrait	Was unwilling to participate in presenting their picture	Willing to participate in presenting, could speak clearer and did not make eye contact with the audience	Willing to participate in presenting, spoke clearly and made eye contact	Willing to participate in presenting, spoke clearly, made eye contact and asked the audience if they had questions	

Assessment, Activity #10

Outcome	Criteria				Total
	1 (Not yet)	2 (Meets)	3 (Fully Meets)	4 (Exceeds)	
Complete all 4 pages of their gratitude card	Left one or more pages of their gratitude card blank	All 4 pages have at least 1 thing added for the recipient.	All four pages have 2 or more things added for the recipient, front cover coloured	All four pages have 2 or more things added for the recipient, and more than 1 reason why they are grateful to have the recipient in their life, front cover coloured	

Assessment, Activity #12

Outcome	Criteria				Total
	1 (Not yet)	2 (Meets)	3 (Fully Meets)	4 (Exceeds)	
Complete all 4 pages of their Gratitude Mini-Book	Left one or more pages of their mini-book blank	All 4 pages have at least 2 things added, their name written on cover page but didn't add any color or element of art	All 4 pages have 2 or more things added, their name written on cover page and drew a picture adding at least one element of art	All 4 pages have 3 or more things added, their name written on cover page and drew a picture adding one or more elements of art	
Demonstrated good speaking/presenting skills during class share of Gratitude Mini-Book	Was unwilling to participate in presenting Gratitude Mini-Book	Willing to participate in presenting, could speak clearer and did not make eye contact with the audience	Willing to participate in presenting, spoke clearly and made eye contact.	Willing to participate in presenting, spoke clearly, made eye contact and asked the audience if anyone had questions.	

Grateful Jake

by Emily Madill

Grateful Jake by Emily Madill

art by Izabela Bzymek, visit www.emilymadill.com for more info

Grateful Jake by Emily Madill

art by Izabela Bzymek, visit www.emilymadill.com for more info

Grateful Jake by Emily Madill

art by Izabela Bzymek, visit www.emilymadill.com for more info

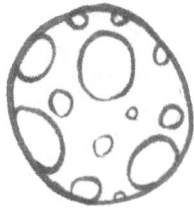

Grateful Jake
by Emily Madill

art by Izabela Bzymek
www.emilymadill.com for more info

Grateful Jake by Emily Madill

art by Izabela Bzymek
www.emilymadill.com for more info

About the Captain Joe Series

The Captain Joe Series was designed as a tool for adults to teach children about constructive imagination. The four books are a fun and interactive way to introduce the concept of "Thoughts Turn Into Things" (so choose the ones that make you happy) to young children, ages five to nine years.

Joe and his thought-zapping superpower will invite children to use their imaginations to constructively choose thoughts that promote healthy self-esteem and self-awareness. Each story is designed to teach a key concept.

Children will be captivated by Joe and his encounter with Wilfred the friendly wizard. Wilfred presents Joe with a special wand that helps him take charge of his thoughts by ZAPPING away his unhappy thoughts and replacing them with ones that are happy.

The introductory story, **Captain Joe to the Rescue** is a great way to begin discussions with children around thoughts, attitudes and personal power in shaping them.

The second story, **Captain Joe Saves the Day** is a great way to open discussions around the importance of following our dreams in an appealing way kids will relate to.

The third story, **Captain Joe's Gift** is a great way to introduce discussions with children around standing up against bullying and celebrating our differences.

The fourth story, **Captain Joe's Choice** is a great introduction to discussions around the power of our thoughts and choices in creating our happiness.

About the author

Emily lives on Vancouver Island, BC with her husband and two sons. She has a degree in Business and Psychology. Emily believes in the importance of teaching children accountability and empowerment from a young age. She enjoys writing and creating anything that will inspire others to believe in themselves. Being a mother is the most creative job she has had to date.

Books by this author:

Captain Joe to the Rescue! (paperback)
Captain Joe Saves the Day! (paperback)
Captain Joe's Gift! (paperback)
Captain Joe's Choice (paperback)
The Captain Joe Collection (hardcover)
Captain Joe Teaching Resources (paperback)

Grateful Jake (paperback)
Grateful Jake (hardcover)
Grateful Jake (iPad edition with audio)
Grateful Jake Resource Guide (paperback)
Grateful Jake Resource Guide (iPad edition)

Emily's books are available for purchase through her distributor Red Tuque Books, and from online sellers such as Amazon around the world.

Emily is also available for hire as a freelance writer and specializes in inspirational articles. She also focuses on fun ideas and activities to boost children's confidence on her Confident Kids are Cool blog. For samples of Emily's writing please visit her blogs.

For more information visit www.emilymadill.com